MW01628435

SIMON THE SWAN

'I wonder what has happened to that swan?'

SIMON THE SWAN

A sequel to
The Lord of the Rushie River

Written and Illustrated by

CICELY MARY BARKER

BLACKIE

First published in 1988 by
Blackie and Son Ltd, 7 Leicester Place, London WC2H 7BP

British Library Cataloguing in Publication Data
Barker, Cicely Mary, *1895-1973*
Simon the swan.
I. Title
823'.912[J]

ISBN 0-216-92455-3

Designed by Malcolm Smythe

Typeset in Bembo by Dorchester Typesetting Group

Printed in Italy

Contents

The swan family

CHAPTER 1
THE SWAN FAMILY

John Swan, the Lord of the Rushie River, and his wife Penninah were swimming slowly up and down, watching their half-grown children, and talking about them as parents do. The cygnets' names had been chosen for them by their friend Susan, the Ferryman's daughter. Penninah was proud of this; she was proud, too, of her strong, clever husband, and wondered which of the young ones would take after him.

"It won't be Timmy," she said. "He is so small and shy. Brownie is a naughty, quarrelsome bird at present, but he is bold and brave, and so is Matilda; one of them might do something notable. No doubt Jane will marry early; she will be a beautiful swan when she gets her white plumage. As for Simon, he thinks of nothing but gobbling water-weed. He will grow up a dunce if he keeps his head under water so much, and never looks about him."

"Time will show," replied John Swan wisely. "Come, my dear, let us go and see what Susan is doing."

As the two swans sailed away, Simon brought his head up from under the water, and shook the drops from it. He had heard all that his mother had said.

"If I *do* eat a lot, isn't that the way to grow to be a big, fine swan?" he said to himself. "Why shouldn't I be as handsome and clever as my Father, and braver and bolder than Matilda, or Brownie, or any of them? I know what I'll do to show I'm not as stupid as they think – I'll fly away and see the world, and come back a famous swan. There's nothing to stop me!"

That very night, when his brothers and sisters were asleep, Simon glided out from among the rushes into the moonlight, then spread his wings and flew over the quiet village of Rushiebanks, towards the hills.

He was a very foolish Swan.

CHAPTER 2
The Dewpond

The grassy hill-tops stretched for miles in the autumn sunshine where Daniel, the old shepherd, went slowly with his flock of sheep, his good dog Patch, and his young friend Roger.

There was no one like old Daniel, who knew so much about living things, and even understood the speech of birds and beasts. Roger longed to learn the secret, and understand too. For there *was* a secret; if you carried with you one little flower from among the many which grew on the hills, you would be able to talk with all the creatures, Daniel said. But when Roger begged to know which flower it was, Daniel would only answer, "Ah, that's telling!"

"Look," said Daniel, pointing upwards. "That's uncommon – that's a swan flying over. He's going slow, as though he's tired."

"He's coming down!" cried Roger.

"So he is! He must have spied that dewpond over there, and be making for it. Creep quiet, not to frighten him, and have a look."

Long ago, dewponds were hollowed out from the hard chalk which lies under the turf of southern hills. They hold the dew and the rain, and never dry up, so that there is always water on the hill-tops for the sheep.

Sure enough, when Roger stole up to the little pond, there was the swan, resting on the water and drinking thirstily.

"Is that a swan?" Roger whispered to Daniel, who had followed him. "Swans are white, aren't they? Not grey like that one!"

"He's a swan right enough, but a young one. He'll get his white feathers when he is grown up, and his dark beak will be red then."

"It's a funny thing," said the shepherd, "– a swan on a dewpond! I've seen a fox drinking there, and many a bird, but never a swan before. Hey, young chap!" he called to the swan. "Have you lost your way?"

The swan (who, you will have guessed, was Simon) looked round and chattered with his beak.

"He says he is seeing the world," said Daniel, then, to the swan, "you go home again, my lad. You're too young, and this is no place for swans. Oh; he says he won't. There! He's off again!"

As Daniel spoke, Simon rose from the pond, and flew on. Roger gazed after him; but now the shepherd was looking at the sky. Clouds were gathering, and the wind was rising.

"There's a storm coming," he said. "We must bring the sheep down to the fold."

CHAPTER 3
The Storm

The dog Patch gathered the sheep together, and they turned towards home, but before they reached the foot of the hill, where the shepherd's cottage stood, the rain had begun, the trees were waving their branches wildly, and the air was full of flying leaves.

"Run on in, while I get the sheep folded," said Daniel. "Your mother won't want you soaked to the skin." Roger ran to the cottage and the shepherd's kind old wife dried him. By-and-by the shepherd came in, shaking the rain from his hat and from the sack he had put round his shoulders, and she bustled about to make tea.

"Mother will guess I'm with you," said Roger, sitting contentedly by the fire. "But I wonder what has happened to that swan?"

"Oh, it was a foolish swan!" said Daniel, shaking his head as he stirred his tea.

At last, when it was nearly dark, Daniel went to the door and looked out, and said that the storm was over.

He fetched his lantern, and lit it.

"I'm going to see that all's well at the fold," he said, "but I'll take you home first."

Outside, the ditches and cart-ruts were like rivers; leaves and branches from the trees were strewn everywhere,

There lay poor Simon, wet, muddy and exhausted.

and there were great puddles across the lane. Roger went slipping and splashing along, so very soon Daniel picked him up and carried him on his shoulder. They had turned a bend in the lane, and were in sight of Roger's home, when they saw, in the dusk, a man coming towards them.

"It's Daddy, looking for me!" cried Roger.

The man stopped suddenly, and bent to look at something on the ground; then straightening himself, he shouted, "Hey, Daniel, bring your lantern here!"

The shepherd set Roger down, and hurried forward, calling out, "What is it?"

"It's a swan; I can't see if it is alive or dead!" shouted Roger's father, Tom Snow, the Squire's gardener.

"A swan!" gasped Roger, following as best he could.

Wet, muddy, and exhausted, there lay poor Simon, with the two men bending over him. At the light of the lantern he opened his eyes.

"He's *not* dead!" cried Roger.

"Looks like the one we saw on the hills today," said Daniel, "but he wasn't coming this way. He must have been blown off his course."

"He's been battered by the storm, that's sure," said Roger's father. "I'll carry him into one of the outhouses, and maybe he'll revive."

He lifted the swan into his arms; Simon was too weak to struggle.

"Thank you kindly for taking care of my youngster, shepherd," said Tom. "Come on, Roger, we'll get some straw and make a bed for the swan, then ask Mother for some warm bread and milk for him."

CHAPTER 4
The Doleful Swan

The Squire's lady heard about Simon, and came to look at him as he lay in the outhouse by the gardener's cottage, on his straw bed, with Roger keeping watch beside him.

Each day she asked, "And how is the invalid this morning, Thomas?" and when on the third day the gardener replied, "Much better, Madam; I think he will soon be ready to fly," she exclaimed:

"But I don't want him to fly! I have often wished we had a swan on the lake here at Heronshaw; they are such stately birds. Cannot we keep him?"

"Why yes, Madam," said Tom. "I can clip his wings so that he can't fly away; and try him on the lake."

So, before long, Simon was swimming to and fro on the beautiful lake. There were water-lilies at one end of it, and tall trees around it; at one side of it were the Squire's house and lawns; on the other side were tall trees, and beyond the trees were the hills.

"How grand," thought Simon, "to be the only swan in such a place!"

But soon he found himself very lonely without his brothers and sisters. The coot and moorhens on the lake were afraid of him and kept out of his way.

And what of his fine plans to see the world? With his

wing-feathers clipped, so that he could not fly, he thought he must stay on that lake for the rest of his life.

The Squire and his wife were puzzled to see their swan looking so doleful. But the Squire said: "Depend upon it, my dear, when spring comes we shall see a change in him! He will cheer up then. Don't worry."

Roger could not visit him as often as he wished, for his mother said, "You'll annoy the Squire if you are always hanging around the lake." But when he did go, Simon seemed to like his company.

"If only I had that magic flower," thought Roger, "I could talk to him and find out why he looks so sad."

This is a short chapter. Nothing else happened for a long time. Simon thought that nothing *could* happen.

But it did.

CHAPTER 5
Roger the Shepherd

Winter had come, and gone again; and it was lovely spring. There were daffodils and primroses beside the lake, and the bare trees began to grow green again with new leaves. But Simon still looked doleful. His feathers and beak were still dull grey, though his beak was not so dark as before. He was still lonely.

Roger could not pay much attention to him; he was spending nearly all his time with Daniel among the lambs. The tiny ones and their mothers were in warm sheltered lambing-pens, but the flock with the older lambs was taken each morning onto the slopes of the hills.

Then, one day, the shepherd slipped when he was moving a heavy hurdle, and twisted his ankle badly.

He was very vexed.

"I can hobble about among the pens and see to the little 'uns," he said, "but those sheep do need to be taken on the hills, and that's what I can't do for a bit. I don't know what's best. If I ask the Squire to spare me one of his farm chaps, well, they don't know the ways of the sheep."

"I know the ways of the sheep! Let *me* take them!" said Roger.

"You! You're a little 'un yourself!" said old Daniel. He looked hard at Roger. "But I think you're a little 'un to be trusted, more than some of the big fellows that can't tell one sheep from another and don't care either. It wouldn't be many days, and Patch would help you. See what your Dad says."

Roger rushed home. At first his parents thought him far too young to be trusted with the Squire's sheep, but in the end they gave way.

"If Shepherd thinks you can do it, well, he knows best," said the gardener; and Mrs Snow said:

"At all events it's fine weather, so you won't come to harm, if you mind what Daniel tells you, and don't go doing anything silly."

Early next morning, Roger was ready. His dinner, and a bottle of milk, were in Daniel's own satchel, slung across his shoulder; and Daniel's crook was in his hand. Its staff was far too long for him, but he was bent on taking it; he was sure the sheep would never think him a proper shepherd without it.

Daniel moved the hurdle from the entrance of the fold, and out came the sheep. Patch ran around keeping them together, and off they all started, up the narrow path to the hillside. Old Daniel watched them go.

"He'll do all right," he said to himself, and limped back to his hut to warm some milk for a weak little lamb that had to be fed from a bottle like a baby.

They moved slowly, higher and higher.

CHAPTER 6

The Magic Flower

Up the winding path, through thickets of hazel and hawthorn trees went the little shepherd with his flock. When they came out on the open hillside, the sheep began to crop the sweet fresh grass as they went slowly higher and higher, until Roger thought they had gone far enough. He looked back and could see, below, the lambing-pens and the three tall fir trees by the shepherd's cottage, and the blue smoke from the chimney.

Larks were singing, out of sight, as he sat down to watch the sheep. Patch sat beside him, ready to go off at a word to fetch back any which strayed too far.

Presently Roger began to pick some of the flowers that grew in the grass, to take home to his mother. Near the gorse bushes, where the turf was nibbled short by rabbits, big dog-violets grew; and in the longer grass on the slopes were early cowslips, and other flowers whose names he did not know. He had a bit of string in his pocket, so he tied them into a little posy, and stuck it in the front of his coat.

Then he thought it was time for dinner. He opened the satchel and spread out the red handkerchief in which his mother had wrapped a big pile of sandwiches and a piece of fruit cake.

Patch, who was sitting beside him, said, "That looks

'That looks very good. Is there any for me?'

very good. Is there any for me?"

Roger stared at him. At the same moment, a skylark rose from the grass quite near him, and went singing upwards. He heard what it sang:

"High, high, high!
To the sky! to the sky!"

Roger was startled, almost frightened. But Patch was wagging his tail in his usual friendly way, and sniffing towards the sandwiches, and Roger threw his arms around him and hugged him.

"Oh Patch, dear old Patch, have I found the magic flower? Can we really talk to each other now?"

"Looks like it, little master; but don't forget your dinner, and don't forget the sheep!" replied Patch.

As he ate, Roger looked again and again at his little posy. Which flower was the one? He could not tell. Had he, perhaps, picked one of them from a fairy ring, without noticing?

But it was a marvellous day. Roger understood what the sheep said to each other, and what the rooks were calling as they flew over. When the sun began to go round to the west, and the shadows grew longer, he sent Patch to gather the flock together, and they started downwards.

As they went, Roger picked another posy for his mother, with primroses and bluebells from the hazel woods.

He meant to keep his first one always, as long as he lived.

"And now I shall be able to talk to that poor swan," he said to himself.

CHAPTER 7
WHERE IS RUSHIEBANKS?

Each day until Daniel's ankle was well Roger took out the sheep, and with Patch's help brought them safely back.

But at last he was free to have his talk with Simon.

When he heard the swan's story, Roger asked: "Where is Rushiebanks?"

"Far away, but I can't tell where," said Simon sadly. "I lost my way in that storm. I shall never be a famous swan now, or even see my brothers and sisters again."

"But won't you grow new wing feathers some day? Then you will be able to fly again, and see the world, or go home if you'd rather."

"I should be afraid. There might be another storm. And if I went home they might jeer at me and drive me away. No, I must stay here; but please come and talk to me sometimes."

"If the other swans knew where you were, one of them might come and fetch you home, and be kind. We might let them know," said Roger thoughtfully.

He asked several birds whether they knew Rushiebanks. The swallows did; they came that way from over the sea, but now they were far too busy with their nests and babies to take a message there.

Roger could not think of any other way to tell the swans

'I shall never be a famous swan now.'

about Simon. Then, one day in early summer, he made a discovery.

Daniel had left the sheep grazing that day in one of the lower pastures, and Roger went with him over the hills to High Farm, where he had business to do. Roger had never been there before.

When the errand was done they stood looking from the brow of High Mount, over miles of green meadows where a river wound its way; near the foot of the hill Roger could see the roofs of a village, clustered by a bridge.

"What's that place?" he asked, pointing to it.

"Why, that's Rushiebanks," answered the shepherd.

"*Rushiebanks*! Oh! Our swan came from Rushiebanks. He said it was a great way off."

"It's no great way. That swan must have flown round about, and thought he came further than he did. Look, there's the carrier's cart, the one that passes Lane End."

Along a white road, far below, went a covered cart, looking like a little toy. Roger watched until it was out of sight; then he said:

"The swan says he lived by the ferry. Where's that?"

"Where you see the cottages, a bit further down the river. Further still, there's Rushiemouth. Look at that bright line out there! That's the sea, that is!"

Daniel pointed, and in the distance Roger saw a silvery streak. He had never seen the sea before.

As Daniel and he turned for home, the old shepherd looked down at him and said:

"So you've been talking to Squire's swan, have you? When did you find that flower, eh?"

Roger shook his head, with a grin.

"That's telling," he said.

CHAPTER 8
"Over the Hills and Far Away"

A few days later, when Roger's mother came downstairs in the morning, she found his slate on the kitchen table, with some large straggly writing on it:

I HAVE HAD BREKFUST AND GON ON THE HILLS.
LOVE FROM ROGER.

"That boy!" she said to her husband. "I suppose he's with Daniel; that's all he seems to think of – being out with the sheep. I wonder whether the others heard him go." (For Roger was the youngest but one of five children.)

"He'll be hungry long before dinner-time, going off like that without his porridge," Mrs Snow went on regretfully. "I'd have given him something to take with him if I'd known."

"Don't you worry," said Tom Snow. "Shepherd'll see to him."

But Roger was not with Daniel. He was going gaily over the hills, quite alone, on his way to Rushiebanks.

He felt so free, without even Patch and the sheep, that he ran, and sang, and called out to the birds and rabbits in the fresh morning air. The dew was still on the grass, and thin mists lay over the quiet fields below him.

But by the time he had passed High Farm and begun to

go down to the steep hillside, the sun was hot, and the way much further than it had looked from above. He was hungry, too; he had only had a piece of bread and a drink of milk before leaving home, and that was a long time ago.

But he plodded on, down a long lane with high hedges, until he came to a finger-post by a stile. One finger, pointing down the lane, said "TO RUSHIEBANKS"; the other, pointing to a footpath across the fields, said "TO THE FERRY".

Roger climbed the stile, and followed the footpath which brought him at last to the river bank, where rough steps led down to the water's edge. On the other side of the river were two or three cottages, and some boats moored by the bank; and on the bank sat a little girl, knitting, with a white nanny-goat tethered near her. On the river a little way to Roger's right were some swans.

The girl looked up, and seeing the small, hot boy, standing and staring around him, called: "Do you want to come over?"

"No, thank you," shouted Roger; and he turned and walked along the bank towards the swans. Now that he was really there, he wasn't sure how to begin; so he sat down and watched them for a while. One of the swans was unusually large, two were pure white; the rest were greyish, like his friend at Heronshaw.

Presently he said: "Is this where Simon came from?"

At once they all gathered near.

"I am his mother," said the smaller of the white swans. "He flew away, too young, and we never saw him again! What do you know of him?"

Roger told the whole story.

When he had finished, the large swan said severely: "Simon is a very foolish bird, though he is my son, and I am the Lord of the Rushie River."

"He is very lonely and sad," said Roger. "I thought if you knew, one of you would come, and maybe bring him home, when his new wing-feathers have grown – though I don't *want* him to go away. I like him very much."

The Lord of the Rushie River said nothing; but one of the young ones ventured to ask: "Where *is* Heronshaw?"

"Over there," replied Roger, pointing to the hills. "I'm sure any heron would show you the way; they come for miles to fish in our lake. *Do* say you'll come!"

The swans were silent.

"Won't you even give me a message for Simon? When I've come all the way on purpose?" pleaded Roger.

"You may tell Simon that if he wishes to come home, I shall not forbid him; but I am not coming to fetch him," said John Swan; and he turned and swam away with great dignity.

Penninah lingered a moment to say hastily: "Please give him my love!" and then she and the young swans followed dutifully behind their Lord.

Roger was left alone.

CHAPTER 9
New Friends

Susan put down her knitting, untied a small boat, and rowed herself across the river. She tied the boat to a stake by the steps and came towards Roger as he sat rubbing his knuckles in his eyes to try to keep from crying. He seemed to have done so little good; and what a long way it would be to go home!

He looked up, and saw Susan. She was a little older than Roger, and had a nice friendly face.

"Won't you come over and sit with me while I mind the ferry?" she said. "I do want to know about you and the swans. It's not everybody who understands swan-talk as I see you do."

So Roger went with her; and as they sat together on the bank, Susan listened with great interest to his story. She had wondered, often, what could have become of Simon.

"I know John Swan very well," she said. "Once he's got an idea in his head, he doesn't like changing it, but I'll talk to him and try and make him see that Simon was *brave* to go off as he did, and is a son to be proud of, even if he was a bit foolish too. Then everything will be all right. Now tell me some more things. Have you any brothers and sisters?"

"Oh yes!" said Roger. "There's Hannah – she helps with Squire's children, and Dick – he's the clever one with books,

Susan listened with great interest to his story.

Ned – he's garden-boy with Dad, then there's me, and then Polly. She's only four."

"I wish I had some brothers and sisters! But I've only got little Snoo for company," said Susan, looking affectionately at the white goat, who gave a little bleat in reply.

"It's a very pretty goat," said Roger, "but what a funny name!"

"Well, you see, we called her Snowflake when she was a tiny kid; but Young William's baby girl couldn't say that, and called her Snoo, and now we all do."

"Who is Young William?" asked Roger.

"He's the son of Old William, who was Ferryman here before Daddy. Young William lives in that cottage next to ours; he's a carpenter; and his wife helps Daddy and me with cooking and washing."

"Haven't you got a mother?" asked Roger.

"No," said Susan. "I don't remember her at all."

Just then a man's voice called out, "Ahoy there! Dinner's ready!"

Susan jumped up.

"That's Daddy!" she said. "You must have some dinner with us. I know he'll say so."

She led the way to the nearest cottage. At the door stood Jim the Ferryman, grey-haired and kindly. He smiled down at Roger and said, "Who's your young friend, Sue?"

She explained; and soon Roger was sitting at the table, enjoying what seemed to him the nicest dinner he had ever had in his life. The Ferryman sat where he could keep an eye on things through the open door.

"You don't seem to have many people come to your ferry," Roger remarked.

"Market days are busy," said the Ferryman, "and

Roger said good-bye to Little Snoo.

mornings and evenings, when people come to and from work."

Then he talked of the river, and the sea (for he had been a sailor) and Susan pointed out one of the boats in which she and her father went, sometimes, all the way to Rushiemouth.

"What an adventure," thought Roger.

"That boat was the *Saucy Sue* when I bought her," said the Ferryman, "but I changed the name. She's the *Faithful Sue* now. Shall I tell you why?"

Roger nodded, and the Ferryman went on, "Because my own Sue never forgot to watch for me, all the time I was away on my last long voyage. Now my man, you've a tidy step to go. If you've had enough, you ought to be off." Then a thought struck him, and he said, "No, it's too far for you to walk back over the hills; Susan shall go along with you to Rushiebanks and see you on the carrier's cart. It will be leaving the bridge in less than an hour, and it passes the lane to Heronshaw."

"Won't the carrier want paying?" asked Roger.

"Susan shall see to that; it won't be much," said the Ferryman.

As they started out, Roger remembered his manners.

"Thank you very much, Mr——" he began, then stopped, and looked at Susan.

"Perry," she said.

Roger began again.

"Thank you very much, Mr Perry, for my nice dinner."

"You were very welcome, Roger. Good luck to you, and come again," said the Ferryman, lighting his pipe.

Roger said good-bye to Little Snoo, and the Ferryman watched the children go.

CHAPTER 10
Home Again

Dragon-flies darted about in the sunshine along the river-path. As the two children came near the place where the swan family were spending the afternoon, Susan whispered, "You'd better say good-bye to John Swan. He likes people to be polite."

So Roger touched his hat, and called out: "Good day to you, John Swan, sir. I'm going home now." And the great swan bent his head in acknowledgement.

"I do think it's funny," said Roger, as Susan and he went on together, "that Mr *Perry* minds the *ferry*. It's like a song! Couldn't you make one about it?"

"I can't make songs! Can you?" said Susan, laughing.

"Old Daniel can, and tunes to play on his whistle-pipe to the sheep," said Roger; and then he had to tell Susan about Daniel, and Patch, and the sheep.

So the time passed happily until he had said good-bye to Susan, and was in the very same carrier's cart, jogging along the same road, that Daniel had pointed out to him from High Mount.

"Mr Perry minds the ferry –" Roger murmured the words over to himself as his head began to nod, and soon he was fast asleep, and never woke until he found the carrier lifting him down from the cart, and saying, "Here's your turning, Sonny."

He stood in the road, bewildered for a moment; then turned and ran up the lane which led home. His brother Ned was at the gate.

"Oh, there you are!" said he. "You're going to catch it, this time!"

And so he did; for Tom Snow had happened to see old Daniel early in the day, and found that Roger was not with him. As the hours went by Mr and Mrs Snow had grown anxious.

Roger stood hanging his head while they scolded him.

"If you go off again, all day, without asking, there'll be a whipping for you," said his father.

"You're too young to go so far alone," went on Mrs Snow. ("That's like what the mother swan said about Simon!" thought Roger.) "Supposing those people hadn't been so kind, what would you have done? And the naughtiest part was making us think you were with Daniel when you weren't.

"Now, eat your supper and go to bed. I don't want any more talk tonight."

Oh dear! Roger, thinking things over in bed, knew quite well that he had been wrong to slip off, making his parents think he was with the sheep. But would they understand why he wanted so much to visit the swans at the ferry?

The door opened gently, and his mother was bending over him.

"You won't do it again, will you dearie?" she said.

Then Roger's arms were round her neck, and he was saying how sorry he was; she tucked him in and a few minutes later he was sound asleep.

CHAPTER 11
A Free Swan

Next morning Roger went to the lake, to tell all that he had seen and heard. Simon was grateful, but still sad.

"You have done all this for me," he said, "but what of all the grand deeds *I* meant to do? I am ashamed."

Roger sat thinking; then he said:

"I don't believe anyone does grand deeds on purpose, anyway, not swans or sheep. I've seen a mother sheep, when a stranger came near; all the other sheep ran away, but she stood by her little new lamb and stamped her foot, and looked fierce, which was really brave for a sheep. But she did it to take care of her baby; not to be grand. You'll be a brave, fine swan, all in good time; after all, you haven't grown up yet!"

Simon considered this; then he said humbly:

"You are very wise, little master. I've been a foolish swan – I see it now."

As he spoke they both looked up. A partly white and partly grey swan, like Simon, was circling overhead, then dropped on the lake, calling out, "Brother, is it you?"

Simon swam rapidly to meet him.

"Brother, it is! Oh my brother, it's surely not little Timmy who has come to find me? Timmy who always wanted to stay at home?"

It *was* Timmy. He said, "I came to tell you that you need not be afraid to come home. Susan has talked to the Lord of the River, and he is ready to be proud of you now. Spread your wings, and let me see if your flying-feathers have grown again."

Simon stretched them out and it was plain to see that the clipped feathers had been replaced by new, strong, white ones. He was a bigger bird than Timmy.

"Why Simon, you are a free swan! Rise up with me, and fly!" cried Timmy.

Roger watched breathlessly as they flew across the surface of the lake, then soared into the air. Soon they were back again; and for the rest of the day they swam about together, going for short flights every now and then. When night came, they settled down together on the bank.

The Squire's lady was delighted; her swan had a companion and was happy at last. But next morning, when she looked out of her window, she saw that there were no swans on the lake.

No one had seen them go; and after a time she gave up expecting them to return.

"I suppose I ought to have clipped his wings again, Madam," said Tom the gardener.

"No, Thomas," said his lady. "I'd rather the swan was free and happy than moping here against his will. Perhaps we shall have another, some day."

CHAPTER 12
An Invitation

The summer months had gone by.

One autumn day, Roger and little Polly stood by the gate, while two new bee-hives were unloaded from the carrier's cart. Ned was helping his father with them, when the carrier turned to Roger and handed him a letter.

"Young lass from the ferry asked me to give you that," he said.

Roger rushed indoors to his mother and tore it open. It was clearly written.

> "Dear Roger," (it said)
> "We are going to Rushiemouth in the boat next Thursday. Would you like to come? If you would, please come with the carrier on Wednesday, and spend the night with us, so we can start early. Then you could sleep here again on Thursday night and go home on Friday. Daddy hopes your mother will let you come, and so do I.
> With love from Susan."

After much talk, the Snows decided to let Roger go. He could hardly believe it!

"Fancy those folks thinking of our Roger, after all this time," said his mother.

She and little Polly saw him off from Lane End. He had his night things in a neat parcel, and Mrs Snow handed a basket up to him in the cart. She had packed it carefully with presents for the Perrys – rock-cakes and a pot of bramble jelly and four beautiful pears.

"Mind how you carry it," she said.

The cart started off, stopping now and then at farms and cottages, to leave or pick up bundles and packages of all kinds. Roger was wide awake this time, and interested in everything he saw.

At last they were at Rushiebanks, and there was Susan, waiting by the bridge.

"You've really come!" she cried.

Roger was glad to hand over the basket to her; and as they set out along the river path, he asked eagerly, "How's Simon?"

Susan stared at him.

"Simon? I haven't seen him. He didn't come home. Timmy flew away the day after you were here, and he hasn't come back either. Aren't they on your lake, then?"

Roger told her what had happened.

"I felt sure I should see him here," he said, looking very disappointed.

"Well," said Susan, "it *is* time now for young swans to leave home. Brownie and Matilda and Jane are all living further down the river, with some other young ones. I do wonder where Simon and Timmy can be!"

She told Roger that her father had to go to Rushiemouth next day about a new ferry-boat. She and Roger could amuse themselves while he was busy. Young William

She and Little Polly saw him off.

would take charge of the ferry while they were gone. Roger had brought a bright shilling with him, to spend at Rushiemouth. He told Susan, "Squire gave it to me for minding his sheep when Daniel hurt his ankle. It has been in my money box all this time."

"People give me pennies sometimes, when I run to fetch Daddy to the ferry-boat. I'll open my money box tonight," said Susan.

CHAPTER 13
THE FAITHFUL SUE

Roger slept that night in the Ferryman's own bed. It was great fun next morning to step on board the *Faithful Sue*, and wave good-bye to the group on the bank: Young William and Young William's pretty wife, and their tiny girl, who clasped her arms round the white goat's neck and called out, "I will take care of Little Snoo!"

The Ferryman took the oars, and down the river they went, past overhanging willows and the place where the young swans were living (but Timmy and Simon were not there), through green meadows where cattle grazed. When the river widened the Ferryman left off rowing and put up his brown sail.

Susan knew how to help; when the Ferryman gave Roger, too, a rope to hold, he held on with all his might, thrilled to feel the tug of the breeze in the sail.

After a time the Ferryman brought out sandwiches and Mrs Snow's rock-cakes, and rosy apples. Now they were passing flat muddy banks, where strange long-legged birds ran, and the river was very wide, with little waves on it.

"We're nearly there!" said Susan.

The harbour at Rushiemouth was full of boats, some lying anchored on the mud, for the tide was low. Away beyond a stone pier was the open sea.

They waved good-bye from the Faithful Sue.

The Ferryman brought the *Faithful Sue* to the quay. He threw a rope, which a man caught and made fast, and Susan went nimbly up a little ladder against the side of the quay. She was used to this, but Roger did not like the look of it at all, with the green water lapping beneath. The Ferryman may have guessed how he felt, for he said: "Up you go, Roger, but take your time. I'm here behind you, to catch you if you slip."

Roger did it somehow, scrambling over the top on his hands and knees, and the Ferryman said, "Well done!" Then he went to find the boat builders he had come to see, leaving Susan and Roger to amuse themselves as they liked.

CHAPTER 14
At Rushiemouth

Though Rushiemouth was a small place, there were plenty of things to look at – boat builders' yards, sheds full of oars and sails, fishing-nets and lobster pots, seagulls perching on roofs and chimneys.

The shops in the narrow streets, too, were full of unusual things: rope and fishing-tackle, sea-boots and oilskins. The spending of Roger's shilling took time. At last he decided on a little jug with a picture of a ship on it as a present for his mother, a pennyworth of toffee to share with Susan, and a pink sugar mouse for another penny, to take home for Polly. That left fourpence.

"I want to take Daniel something," he said. "What could I buy for fourpence?"

Then, in a little draper's shop where Susan was buying a blue hair-ribbon for herself he saw the very thing, a pile of large cotton handkerchiefs in gay colours, marked "4^{d} each".

He chose one with green and white patterns; the shop-woman obligingly folded it round the china jug, with the sugar mouse safely inside that, and tied up the parcel with paper and string. Then they came to the toyshop window.

It was a tiny shop, but very full of toys. Susan still had a few pennies left, so she bought a present for Roger – a most beautiful large glass marble, with twisted stripes in it, blue and red and green and yellow.

Then the Ferryman came along and took them to have a meal at the Inn.

Unluckily, the boat-builder he wanted was away from Rushiemouth that day, and would not be back until late in the afternoon.

"We shan't get home till dark, at this rate," said the Ferryman.

"The more fun!" thought the children. They went back to the quay, and Roger was surprised to see how the tide had come up. Boats that had been lying anchored on the mud were all afloat, and there was no longer a deep climb down the little slippery ladder. The Ferryman brought the *Faithful Sue* round to some stone steps, and busied himself stowing away the stores he had been buying. Then he thought it time to look for the boat-builder again.

CHAPTER 15
The Harbour Swans

The sky and the water were pink with sunset, and all the swans had gathered from far and near to one place, where a little stream flowed into the harbour from under an archway.

Roger leaned over a railing to watch. The elder swans were drinking, while the younger waited their turn. One of these looked up, and seeing Roger, swam quickly towards him, saying, "Little master, don't you know me?"

"Why, it's Simon!" cried Roger. "I *didn't* know you, with your feathers all white, and your beak quite pink! Oh, Simon, I never thought I should find you here! Why didn't you go home after all?"

"We did," began Simon. Susan put in:

"I never saw you!"

"Ah, it was early! You were still asleep," said Simon. "We paid our respects to our parents, and flew on. It was Timmy's thought that we should go adventuring together as I had meant to do alone. We have seen strange sights, and learnt many things. He is going home for good, some day; he means to marry a young lady swan and take her with him."

"What shall you do then, Simon?" asked Roger.

Simon wasn't sure. He liked Rushiemouth, he said, and

the company of so many swans.

"If you ever get tired of Rushiemouth, Simon," said Roger, "come back to Heronshaw! Squire's lady was right down sorry to lose you, and so was I. Why are you swans all drinking in this one place?"

Simon explained: "Because this stream is fresh water; we always drink here. The harbour water is too salt to drink."

Then Roger heard the Ferryman calling him and he had to go.

The *Faithful Sue* passed the procession of swans, all making for their sleeping-place, and the children called good-night to Simon and Timmy.

Jim Perry wrapped Susan and Roger in some coats and scarves he had brought with him; it would be cold on the water now the sun was set, and the stars coming out.

Roger, with his hand in his pocket, grasping his precious marble, listened in a kind of dream to the sound of the oars. It was quite dark by the time they reached the ferry; Susan held the lantern while her father tied up the boat.

"I must get you two to bed," he said.

As the Ferryman tucked him up, Roger said sleepily, "I think I'd be a sailor if I wasn't going to be a shepherd."

Next morning the Ferryman was taking people across the ferry on their way to market – women from the farms with baskets of eggs or butter, or a boy with mushrooms to sell.

Roger was eager to get home, to tell his adventures, so that instead of waiting for the carrier's cart that afternoon he determined to walk back over the hills.

Susan went part of the way with him, and with her for company the way across the fields and up the long lane did not seem nearly so far as on that hot day, when Roger first came. When they reached the top of High Mount, the sight of the rolling hills and the far blue distance was as new and wonderful to Susan as the sea had been to Roger.

Then she had to turn homewards, and Roger went on alone, listening to the larks singing overhead. Presently on the breeze came the tinkle of a sheep-bell. Roger ran to the top of a hillock and saw a flock grazing a little way off. He shouted, "Hello!" and next minute Patch was bounding to meet him, and nearly knocking him down with joy.

Daniel was eating his midday bread and cheese by a dewpond. Roger sat down with him. Susan had put some lunch for him in Mrs Snow's basket, but before he ate it he unwrapped the green and white handkerchief and presented it to the shepherd.

"Well, I never!" said Daniel, spreading it out. "This *is* a surprise and no mistake! I'll be real smart with this. To think of you bringing old shepherd a present from Rushiemouth!"

CHAPTER 16

THE LORD OF THE LAKE

Spring had come again, and Roger, long-legged, proud and very happy, was going home after a day among the lambs.

The Squire had come along that day, and had asked whether Daniel would not be glad to have a strong young under-shepherd to help him.

"There's my under-shepherd," said Daniel, pointing at Roger.

"But, handy as he is, he can't do a man's work yet, carrying hurdles, and hay, and mangolds and so on," the Squire had said.

"I don't want a stranger, sir. That boy knows the sheep, and he's growing fast. I'd rather keep on, till he's big enough for the heavy jobs – with your leave, sir."

"What do you say to that, Roger?" asked the Squire.

"Please, sir, it's what I want," answered Roger.

"Then I'll speak to your father, and you shall have a small weekly wage for what you do already, as Ned has for his garden work. By the way," the Squire added, "look at the lake when you go home. Two swans have come here today."

Two swans! Were they Simon and Timmy? Roger would soon see.

He came to the lake and looked. Yes, there they were – a

The Lord of the Lake

large, handsome swan, pure white, with an orange-red beak, and a very graceful smaller one. The large one *was* Simon!

He saw Roger and swam quickly towards him, followed by his wife. She was one of the harbour swans.

Simon said: "We have come to make our home here, where everyone was kind to me when I was young and foolish. My wife is charmed with the lake. I have learned wisdom, little master!"

"And you are a most splendid swan, Simon," said Roger. "Oh, I *am* glad you have come back! I must tell Susan."

He looked round; the Squire's wife was beside him. She had brought bread for the swans, and she laid her hand on Roger's shoulder and said, "I know you understand the swans. Tell me, is one of them our own swan back again? And is the other the one who took him away?"

"The big one is our Simon, Ma'am, and the other is his wife. They are going to stay here always! I think he is about as fine, now, as his father, the Lord of the Rushie River!"

"Then," said the Squire's lady, looking very pleased, "we must call him the Lord of the Lake of Heronshaw!"